Conversation Pieces

Conversation Pieces

BRENDA TAYLOR-HINES

To order additional copies of this book, contact:
Xlibris
844-714-8691
www.Xlibris.com
Orders@Xlibris.com

ISBN: Softcover   979-8-3694-2649-4
         Hardcover   979-8-3694-2648-7
         EBook   979-8-3694-2651-7

Library of Congress Control Number: 2024916138

Print information available on the last page

Rev. date: 01/06/2025

Table of Contents

Acknowledgements

First giving thanks to God for strength and encouragement through the tough times.

A special thank you to my baby sister Yvonne for inspiring and praising me to go on and do it because of my creativity and talent even though it's been thirty years.

To my friends who said, "you are teaching people steps or a process to manage their feelings and creating an opportunity for them to write stories and poems."

Introduction

Conversation Pieces is a compilation of experiences with family members and other people written in poems and a short story. These experiences display a gamut of emotions leaving images etched in my memory to be replayed time and time again. **Conversation Pieces** may trigger pleasant thoughts of similar encounters or stimulate you so you are motivated to explore your creative side. Whatever your response, **Conversation Pieces** is certainly something to talk about. Perhaps you have **Conversation Pieces** in your family too. Think about it!

The poems in **Conversation Pieces** were part of a journal capturing traumatic events, heartbreaks, church conflicts, racisms, women's issues and disappointment. Salutes and acknowledgement to family members for being who they are and encouraging them to excel at whatever they chose to do or become.

Journaling was how I handled conflicts and negativity. It was a therapeutic response that helped me cope, relieve stress, depression and hostility. It was a tool also used with elementary school children to help them deal with their trauma, anxiety and disruptive behavior at a Charter School.

According to research journaling can have a positive effect on your health and mental health. Journaling allowed me to tone down my anger, reduce elevated blood pressure, relax and resolve conflict peacefully. These poems reflect those moods.

Conversation Pieces features an activity called "**The Game.**" It is designed as a friendly activity for family and friends. The purpose of "**The Game**" is for the reader to share his or her interpretation of various poems to other family members in the group. The instructions are simple and easy to follow, play "**The Game.**"

The Gift

The gift arrived today.
No time to open, too busy to care.
So much to do and so little time.
I paused momentarily, then glanced at the package
on the floor.
It seemed to beckon me.
Curious, I opened it.
Confetti fell to the floor.

The textured pages felt smooth against my
fingertips.
Without much thought, I sat down.
I leafed through the pages slowly.
One smile, then another.
One hand overed my mouth.
"Hmm" I said, "the gift arrived today."

For My Son

Be a man, take a stand - don't join others in the band.
Make your own choices, not with mixed voices - go solo if you can.
Dance to the beat of your own drummer, don't get dumb in the crowd.
Sometimes the best music you can make is your own, yes alone,
with your own tone.
Yeah, strength comes in numbers but don't get outnumbered by a
crowded self-interest group who aren't interested in you.
Be a man take a stand for what's right for you.
Don't worry about the crowd, hey let them get loud, taunt and tease you.
Hey, won't that displease you and maybe open your eyes, to their other side.
That's okay, be a man...you can take this.
Yeah, be a man....you don't have to fake it.
Believe in yourself, and just let others make it.

Heir Apparent

Standing in his shadows,
in the background of his life.
Holding on to secrets, that could cause his fall from grace.
Wanting recognition for the deeds you do for him.
More than just a thank you or a pat upon the head.
Desirous of his power which could even be shared.
Vying for his position in a field of many contenders.
Leaves you no choice but to voice your opposition to all others.
In a meeting with your master, you play your final hand.
Sharing all his secrets, you take your final stand.
Tensions mount, tempers flare - the last demand is made.
Abdicate or face disgrace and silence fills the room.
Face to face, eye to eye, he calls this an imposition.
You have no desire to respect his wishes, you yell
"Step down from your position."
The challenge made, the contender wins
and the master yields his crown.
He concedes defeat then slowly turns to say
"Your error is not apparent, but you've worn the crown for years."

Deceptive Practices

Lies and deceit did not spare me the consequences of risky behavior.
Did you care?
Sharing and caring did not spare me pain and shame of deceit.
Did you care?

Blind Lessly trusting, abandoning principles for rites of passion
while wanting to believe, at last, you incapable of deception.
Hollow words echo hope but last as long as a whisper.
Professional ethics espouse principles of rights and wrong, yet
private desires caused us to throw passion to the wind.

When confronted by the truth, I met with more lies that I despised.
Easier to blame others than face reality.
Can't talk to you, won't stalk you.
Just balk at the thought of you.
Need help, got help and medication eased my pain.
Time will heal the hurts and distance will ease my pain.
Solitude is all I gained.

Colored Rage

Women of color, African descent rich in heritage,
strength and pride.
Some strong in resentment toward other women
of color, African descent.
We met on the battlefield of life with the stage
set for conflict with characters drawn
by the controlling hands of others with a
distorted sense of self-worth and importance.
Viewed as sisters, related as rivals, adversaries in
our struggle fighting for limited resources.
Criticizing instead of complimenting.
Tearing down instead of building.
Ostracized by attitudes that cause color lines to form.
Growing weary instead of growing strong.
Stuck in a rut of low self-esteem.
Surviving in cliques and enclaves.
Climbing the ladder while stepping on the toes of those
who made your success possible.
Hostile glares, cold stares await your every turn.
False bravadoes mask our true intentions.
To be equal is threatening, to be less that equal is the norm.
Driven by internal rage, the stage is set for conflict
and humiliation.
Sister against sister.
Your defeat is imminent.
Divided and conquered by those who will turn against her too.

RESCUED

I walked Into the lion's den, prey was all around.
Stares evident, snarls heard and tension filled the air.
No allies in the den, friends were no longer friends.
Their eyes moved with me, their anger was all I could see.
Risks acknowledged and understood, too late to run or hide.
Their intentions clear, terrorize her with fear and teach her a
lesson for her defection.
My thoughts were not on my defeat rather who would rescue me.
Would he be here in time?
Was he a figment of my imagination?
The jacquels turned, the hyenas laughed and the lions roared with glee.
I turned to face the music of this crowd with discontent.
I closed my eyes to brace for their attack while waiting for the
carnage to begin.
Suddenly from out of nowhere, they stood paralyzed in their tracks.
Unable to move or choose their next steps. They stood in silence.
The clouds opened up, the storm quickly began and lighting hit the
trees, the ground and all around the lion's den.
He stood in front of me and approached the hungry crowd.
I kneeled down to pray for God to make me brave today
The situation bleak but I rose to face the challenge and thanked.
God for his intervention.
He said "Go."
I departed without fear of this challenge and the knowledge that God
does not give you more than you can handle.

My Twin

You speak no words, I hear your voice.
I grimace, you feel my pain.
You wonder, I think your thoughts.
I hear your voice, you call my name.
You pick up a pen, I write your words.
I pick up the telephone, you're on the line.
You touch my picture, I feel the warmth.
I awake, you yawn.
Miles apart but still in touch.
Distant but no distance between us.
Identical at birth now mirror images of different views.
Separate but not a part.
Synchronized and in harmony.
Bound by more than a cord but a common accord.
You call my name, I answer.
I grimace you feel my pain.

A Lesson Learned
The Hard Way

You tolerated my indiscretions,
been with me through my pain.
You've listened to my ranting,
with patience and refrain.
You've accepted without judging
some pretty horrible acts.
And through it all you've waited
And now you'll take me back.
Surprised, of course.
Relieved, oh yes.
It's what I've wanted too.
'Cause now I know with all my heart,
I'll never do better than you.

Harassment

HOUNDED BY THE DISBELIEVERS.

HARASSED BY THE MAN.

HUNTED BY HIS SUPPORTERS AND HIS HUNTRESS WIFE.

HUMILIATED BY THE STAFF.

HURT FOR TAKING A POSITION, HASSLED FOR THIS STANCE.

HUMAN WAS THE EXCUSE THEY GAVE.

HEED THE WARNING NOW.

HIDING OUT IN THE DAYTIME.

HEARING VOICES AT NIGHT.

HAVENS NOT AVAILABLE, HAVE NO PLACE TO GO.

HELP IS NOT LIKELY IN THIS PLACE.

HEAVY IS MY PAIN.

HOLDING OUT FOR RESCUE, BUT NO HELP IN SIGHT.

HAVE TAKEN THE POSITION, YES, I'LL STAY AND FIGHT.

HOLLOW IS THE COMPLAINT I'M TOLD.

HYSTERICAL I BECOME.

HELLISH IS THE PLACE I WORK.

HUMANLY TREATMENT IMPOSSIBLE,

AM HEADING FOR THE DOOR.

HOSTILE DEBATES FOLLOW

AND HOODLUMS REIGN SUPREME.

HAVING REACHED THE POINT OF NO RETURN,

I'M FIRED FOR NO CAUSE.

HAPPY THAT IT'S OVER, HUMILIATED NO MORE.

HAVE FOUND THE STRENGTH TO LIVE AGAIN

I AM ON MY OWN ONCE MORE.

Wicked Ways

Engaging eyes, enchanting lies
but your wicked ways still show through.
Desired to be helpful are seen right through, your interest isn't
genuine nor are you.
Deceit is the game you play, disguised as concern.
One-upmanship is what you seek, armed with good intentions
but your approach is weak.
Getting even is your aim, while spreading misery and pain.
No justification needed for your behavior,
Envy and jealousy are the taste you favor.
Driven by false beliefs and unhappiness you pursue others
whose success you believe is more real than your own.
Don't you know, I know your game?
Don't you know, that's why I don't hang with someone with
your wicked ways.

Renaissance of Love

Written off the adventures that love often brings,
still locked in the mind set of avoidance of pain.
But far in the distance, and oblivious to me,
you sought my attention and beckoned my return to the world of love.
Watching and waiting for the appropriate time to pose the question
"will you be mine"?
Reluctant to hear the answer, for fear of rejection.
Anxious for contact, but not a fatal attraction.
Fueled by more than pangs of passion,
But a balance of intellect and attraction.
A twist of fate, not a tryst – capricious, not carnal.
Guided by a shared tomorrow,
incomplete now but on a steady course.
Not a passing fling, but a permanent thing.
A timely renewal culminating and exploring new heights and no lows,
a preview of better things to come.
My response surprised me, but cool heads prevailed.
The past behind us and the future in view.
Committed, caring and with mutual respect we'll guide each other,
Be there for each other and share in the renascence of love.

Smoldering Passion

You said one thing and did another. The lip service was not your only disservice. Your words never matched your deeds. Shaped by your experiences, you spoke half-truths masking lies with smiles, gifts and kindness. It took little to provoke you, even jokes awoke the anger in you. Jack Daniels and coke provided the courage when you spoke, and your cigarette clouded the room from view.

You said trust was a must and whatever you did, you'd always have my best interest at heart. Little did I know that a fire was smoldering fueled by suspicions from your past.

What you liked, now you disliked; what you loved now you hated. It was confusing and I didn't know what to do. Conflict was staged, manufactured to start fights between you and me.

Assurances by me were futile, reassurances were useless as you screamed and hung up the phone. I ignored all the signals, thinking love would prevail but there's a Part of me that has known this relationship was hell.

Based on your perception that I was unfaithful to you, you wouldn't listen, couldn't hear me and the anger turned to rage. Cold was your greeting, there was anger in your eyes. You worked yourself up so everything I said was a lie. I knew a fight was coming but I didn't know when.

I knew I'd be blamed and made to feel ashamed. Infidelity is not the issue, it's the hatred in you. Slapped into reality, staring in disbelief your ranting and raving have only brought you relief.

The physical scars will heal but the emotional ones will linger. Time heals all wounds and though my pain is deep. I rejoice in knowing I am still here to weep.

Be Who You Are

Dare to be different, because you are.
Don't let them push you, stand tall.
Be wary but not afraid.
The debts they make will be paid.
You are special, you are unique.
It's not your fault they can't see beyond their
jealousy and insecurities.
Now, don't weep.
You have family and friends who care.
We are always here, never fear.

Dedicated to my niece, Kristina

Harsh Realities

I started a new job; I relished it with enthusiasm and pride.
Instead, it turned out to be hellish.
I found no one on my side.
I wanted to be a team player, but some folks were people slayers.
I said one thing, they said I said something else.
Instead of working with disenfranchised people disappointed by
failed promises made by leaders, I worked with people without a
vision sought with derision.
My naivete, though refreshing, was quickly abandoned for the
Reality that ideals are destroyed or stolen by those in power.
Awesome I thought.
Who said slavery is over.
Apparently, only the masters have changed.

Isms

Which Ism is it that forms
the basis for your anger?
Which Ism is it that prevents
you from working in this group?
Racism, **sexism** or **Chauvinism**
are the Isms that you face.
Your anger is a stumbling block
too big to hide, its written on your face.
Can you put aside your silly pride and
and join us in this place?
Or will your Isms keep you from
joining the human race?

Rivals

Professionals being unprofessional, street folks talking street.
Vying for positions at a table with many seats.
Each trying to maintain an image that's off balance and indiscreet.
One group says one thing, the other hears a challenge.
Each stalks the other.
Striving for status they play the ego game.
Unnecessary but necessary battle lines are drawn.
Professionals with their rhetoric and street folks with their rage.
Lines drawn; attitudes formed but issues still unclear.
Who will make the first move?
Who will win the prize?
A stalemate is the outcome in this quest for trivial pursuits.
Going nowhere on the road to somewhere, they go their separate ways.

Conflict unresolved to be resolved another day.
Each claiming victory on history is an enigma to us all.

My Eyes

My eyes don't lie, vision clear and focused not contaminated by disease or envy.

My eyes see through the façade and recognize you've kept a hectic pace.

I see your beauty, talent and grace. I see your struggles and conflict that brought you to this place.

I see your pain; it is evident on your face. I see the boundaries you put around your space.

I am enticed, what you present is appealing. I can't hide my affection, it's a reflection of what I am feeling.

I see your desire for better things in life. I see your struggles with people and strife. I see your dreams; they offer love not rejection.

I see the experiences that have made you who you are. are I offer my assistance, so your journey is not as far.

Hoping for Love

Silent reflections give way to fond memories of less complicated times when work schedules and distance were not obstacles to clandestine encounters.

Finding a balance between work and commitments demands reassessing priorities and still settling for phone calls, romantic cards and unkept promises to meet again as promised.

Memories sustain temporarily but absences contribute to doubts about the longevity of our affair.

Our love is not the challenge, finding time to keep it balanced commands efforts, energy and both our talents.

Cravings are never satisfied. Coping is hoping that sincere words were more than gestures, feelings were real, calls will be returned, and deeds were not wilds seeds sown in passion.

Growing UP

Growing up can be a challenge. The key
is to find a balance between school, friends, home and parents.
You know the difference between right and wrong.
You will find your niche; you'll figure out where you belong.
You have feelings, we all do – parents too.
It is okay to get angry but don't lose your perspective and
always be respectful.
Give yourself some time, think before you act.
Patience is more than a virtue, it's a gift you give yourself.
In time you will see things more clearly.
You'll see things aren't so bad.
You may lose some friends while others will remain true.
You'll make some poor choices, we all do.
My advice is to find a caring person you can talk to.
Growing up is a challenge, the key is to find your balance.

Getting Back to Basics

Less impressed by material things.
More inclined to count my blessings.
Caused I've learned some valuable lessons

Some hard, some soft – nothing in between.
Just grown up being wiser not angry or mean.
Trying to put some of the things I have seen in perspective.

Relied on sayings and past traditions to keep me
focused, balanced and on my mission.
Threads woven; seeds sown – getting back to basics
Is where I belong.

Slick Ric and Wild Billy

Slick Ric and Wild Billy, boys but men real silly. Divisive in nature, arrogant in style, each with racist views and possessed a love for women of hues. Slick wore silk and Billy wore leather. One from the south, the other from the east. Together they wove threads of destruction, fueling people's fears with embellishments and lies. Both up to no good, wannabees with few skills. Each worked one job but fancied another.

Disliked Black men but played politically correct games. Angry at the system for being displaced due to affirmative action, they wanted satisfaction for alleged losses due to reverse discrimination.

Delusional and unusual in their approach to people. What they could not conquer they sought to destroy. Spreading rumors and innuendo was their favorite ploy. They turned people against people for the sake of the job. They inflated their worth, citing their dearth of knowledge.

Each craved for attention. Desired men in business and women in bed. Not smooth operators but uncouth negotiators. No line was uncrossed, no tactic unfair, it was all or nothing and it didn't seem unfair.

Their motives were clear but not to the public. They preyed on companies with a line about their work. They didn't do anything phenomenal except take credit for other people's work. Slick set up a company designed to make fast money. Slick was the master and Wild Bill was his tool. Bill was more educated, and Slick was a fool.

Slick wasn't slick and Wild was really. Con men in suites and Casanovas at heart. Practicing deception, they stalked their victims well. People are stupid was their motto and creed. Introduced by their colleagues citing their talents to meet your needs.

People stood back and watched the two do their things. They rambled the rhetoric, tossed each other the ball, dodged the tough questions and raced through the halls. They made elegant promises, showed graphs about trends, bar charts with costs and promotional tools. They shook hands with men, kissed all the women and their babies, and pledged their support while all the time eyeing women in skirts.

Finally, they finished. The crowd was dazzled. "It's in the bag." said Slick. "Oh yeah," cried Billy. They beckoned the leaders to come and make the call. "Do we have the contract? Can we start in the fall?"

"There will be no contract," said the woman in charge. "Oops," said Slick and "Oh no, "said Billy. It was the women they touched when they ran down the hall.

The room became silent. The smiles turned to frowns. With a look that could kill, she said "boys I am not thrilled to have met you. You've made 23 passes, and I don't mean with a ball. You touched inappropriately women in the hall. You've made promises that you can't keep. You've insulted several men by calling them the wrong race. In your haste to close the deal, you offended people with statements in poor taste. You called bar charts graphs, danced the wrong dance and dodged the wrong questions and this is your last."

The guards were summoned and showed them the door. Slick was sad and Wild sullen. Quietly they walked to the car. "What time is it Slick?" It's half past seven. If we hurry, we can still make it to Heaven," said Wild. "Heaven where the hell is that?" said Wild. "It's a place where we might still be able to cut a deal," said Slick.

So off they went in their red corvette playing loud calypso music and shouting obscenities. Who knows their fate further down the road. But one thing for sure, it's a story untold.

THE LAST DANCE

Kind words were heard at first.
Good deeds were received with thanks.
They were all part of the choice I made to be with you.
What I did not see was what you wanted me to be, under your control.
Captivated by your charms, I did not hear nor see the alarms.
This May December romance was not my first dance
but another chance to take the floor again.
I wanted to be your partner.
I accepted your **twists and shouts**, your shuffle around
the tough questions until the last **jerk**.
Confusion reigned **supreme**.
Temptations to leave were real.
I thought it was **just my imagination,** but I stayed for **sentimental reasons.**
When the smoke cleared, I knew it was a **miracle** I survived.
You are no longer **my guy.** I have no sad goodbye only farewell.
If ever I see you again, maybe I will save the last dance for you.

Just Talk

You talked about what you did for me so you could glorify your worth.
You talked about how you did no wrong, to meet your ego needs.
You talked to anyone who'd listen about how you'd even die for me.
You talked about how you lived your life helping others to achieve.
You talked about how you put me first above family and your friends.
What you never talked about was your need to control every facet of my life.
It was not what you said but what you did that caused me to eventually leave.
If you practiced what you preached, you would not have to publicize your ego needs.
No matter how many times you say those words what you say will never be true.
You were the only one impressed with your rhetoric and deceit. Now your friends
are gone and you're all alone, you can't go back but you can move on.

DADDY'S GIRLS

Resilient as pearls.
Diverse hues, intelligent too. Raised in poverty with riches abound.
Written off because of where we lived.
Criticized because we had nothing to give.
Life went on and on we went achieving goals because of common sense.
Education was the car we drove.
Never late, always on time.
Hard working girls from hard working parents.
We weren't sorry, we had get-up and go.
Challenged to be something instead of nothing.
Pushed to excel, cause poverty is hell.
Daddy's girl were survivors in a jungle with many predators and foes.
We went on to achieve 'cause daddy believed that his girls were diamonds in the rough.
We had his temperament, and we were tough.
With egos intact, daddy kept us on track, and we never looked back.
We are daddy's girls, resilient as pearls.

Daddy's Girls Photo

Reflections on the Glass

Another dreary day, another rainy night in Georgia and my thoughts turn to you. Looking out of the window blank stares give way to daydreams and I see your reflections on the glass. Lost in the past, I reminisce about the last time I saw you. We used to talk a lot, we used to laugh a lot and dream about how we would change the world.

Though memories bridge the distance, I cannot forget the fire when you spoke and your silly jokes. Startled by the rain hitting the wndowpane, I smiled and rushed to find an old photograph. Unsuccessful in my search, I settled down to revisit another memory of you and me.

I remember our Afros, platform shoes, our anti-blues attitudes and our peach symbols. I remember the pledge we made, to make our own way. You were my best friend, and we were college buddies. You were always positive and had a lot to give.

As I get up to leave the room, I still see you reflection on the glass. Undaunted I looked across the room and realized the light projected and image from an old, framed photograph of you onto the windowpane. Uncanny I thought, I will always remember your reflection on the glass.

A Parent's Motto: I Won't Give Up On You

I won't give up on you regardless of the silly things you do.

I won't give in to your tirades, despite the headaches your behavior causes.

I won't love you less even though you do not always try your best.

I won't do less for you even though you think I do not do enough.

I won't treat you badly even though you want to be bad.

I won't accept less when more is required and expected.

I won't allow you to give up when you have not done all you can do.

I won't lower my standards when I know you can meet or exceed them.

I won't fight your battles, but I will advise you on strategic moves.

I won't ignore you as you fight through this adolescent phase.

It is not easy being an adolescent but being a parent is no piece of cake.

Our challenge is balance and grow together from all of our mistakes.

Life's Little Challenges

Not always happy with the hand you're dealt.
Can't always see the writing on the wall.
Can't always get up after the fall.
Life's little challenges aren't always a ball.
Can't seem to balance work and play.
Can't seem to find a friend these days.
Haven't been to church but know you need to pray.
The grass seemed greener on the other side.
You jumped the fence then realized they lied.
Not impressed by your decisions, you can't go back and so you go on.
Sometimes you win and sometimes you lose.
Sometimes you can't see the forest for the trees.
Sometimes you can't be all you want to be.
Sometimes life's challenges aren't really clear.
You ponder your next move but with fear.
You burned some bridges you cannot mend.
Angry with yourself but you take it out on others.
Get a grip child, you know you can do better.
Accept the choices you made, learn from your mistakes.
Reach out to others but in a caring way.
Set some goals but do not sway.
Things will get better in time you'll see.
Sure, life's challenges aren't always a ball. ball.
But you can pick yourself up when you fall.

You Bring A Lot to The Party

You bring a lot to the party.

You're kinda hearty.

Your head in the right place, you move at your own pace.

You're aware of what you face, you know you can be replaced.

You left your baggage behind, began this relationship with an open mind.

You were surprised by what you found, a woman who is really down to earth and who keeps you first. You thought you'd have to rehearse your lines and moves. You underestimate your talents, moved in and found your balance. Baby, you forgot you bring a lot to the party.

Anticipation

I suspect you are afraid of me, not in a scary sense but its's the way I make you feel.

I suspect you are unsure of me, in a questioning way, are my motives sincere?

I suspect you are curious, perhaps you are wondering is this woman for real?

I suspect you see the fire in me..... maybe you desire me and want to be fulfilled.

I suspect you want some answers too, to questions about how we really feel.

Just know that we can write the script, be ourselves, this is a sequel and it's so real.

My Sister

My sister reminds me that there will be times when I feel the pain too great, the road too rough and the weight too heavy to carry.

My sister encourages me to remember our childhood and draw on those strengths that saw us through poverty, hunger and illnesses.

My sister reminds me that we are of strong stock, resilient in spirit, relentless in the pursuit of our goals, determined to break barriers, cross roadblocks and create bridges where there were none.

My sister challenges me to go on because I can, to rise above it because I can, to go forward because I can.

My sister reminds me that we are somebody, not doormats to be walked on, but a force to be reckoned with.

My sister smiles and says we are fighters girl. Nobody gives you anything, but people will try to take everything away. Stand tall, and if you fall – get up. You're a fighter girl.

My sister assures me that she is behind me and beside me. Yes, you will feel down girl but never for long. We have a history of strength and a future of challenges. Now get up and go on.

Dedicated to my little sister, Yvonne

Who Are You?

It's not enough just to love me.
It's not enough just to hug me.
I want to know who you are.
I want to know what you stand for.
I'm interested in the depth of your vision. What is your religion?
Do you say the Pledge of Allegiance?
Are you civil with your rights?
Do you go home at night?
Are your views minuscule?
Are you affirmative with your actions?
Or do you say things and later make retractions?
Are you schooled or just cool?
Are you anybody's fool?
Where is your family from?
Do you have a sense of direction?
Are you out for just affection?
Do you fear rejection?
Can you appreciate your mate?
Do you practice what you preach?
Do you want things beyond your reach?
What are your talents?
Are you balanced?
Who are you?

Nicole

Soft spoken and decisive, you let your opinions be known.

Confident and articulate you are heard with clarity and raised eyebrows.

Designed with genes from gifted parents your actions speak for your talents.

Intelligent and determined, you selected a path many others cannot balance.

You rise from a foundation built on strong family values and emerge as focused – no hocus pocus.

Serious and curious, you step out on your own.

Mindful of the risks but certain if you fail your foundation will support you, we always will – just give us a call.

Dedicated to my niece.

INTERPRETATIONS

The poems describe experiences with people, family and social issues. The author's interpretation is described below.

The Gift Arrived Today – reactions to a surprise package.

My Twin – the bond between identical twins.

Colored Raged -an example of conflict that exists between some women.

Deceptive Practices – the consequences of abandoning your values and beliefs.

A Lesson Learned the Hard Way – a person in a relationship learns acceptance.

Harassment – harassment in the workplace.

Wicked Ways – an assessment of a so-called friend.

Renascence of Love – people question what they see and feel before venturing into a new relationship.

For My Son – a mother challenges her son to determine his own destiny.

Smoldering Passion – an abusive relationship.

Heir Apparent – an apprentice awaits impatiently to step into his master's role.

My Sister – one sister reminds another sister of their strength.

Isms – an individual's prejudices.

Rivals – an example of group conflict.

My Eyes – first impressions.

Hoping for Love – starting a new relationship.

Growing Up – the pain and challenge of growing up.

Harsh Realities – workplace conflicts.

Getting Back to Basics – a return to past traditions.

Slick and Wild Billy – an account on the behavior of two flawed individuals.

The Last Dance – an analogy.

Daddy's Girls – childhood resiliency.

Just Talk – the rhetoric of an unhappy ex-friend.

Reflection From the Glass – daydreaming about the past.

Be Who You Area – a declaration to defy so called friends and maintain your integrity and values.

I Won't Give Up On You – a declaration of love from a parent to a child.

Life's Little Challenges – people who blame others for their problems.

Anticipation – a person questioning their feelings.

You Bring A Lot To The Party – a person starting a new relationship.

Who Are You? – an inquiry about a person's values, beliefs and ethics.

Nicole – recognition for a job well done.

Rescued – conflict and a test of faith.

Game Pieces

The Gift	For My Son	Heir Apparent
Deceptive Practices	Colored Rage	Rescued
My Twin	A Lesson Learned The Hard Way	Harassment
Wicked Ways	Renaissance of Love	Smoldering Passion
Be Who You Are	Harsh Realities	Isms
Rivals	My Eyes	Hoping for Love
Growing UP	Getting Back to Basics	Slick and Wild Billy
The Last Dance	Just Talk	Daddy's Girls
Reflections on the Glass	A Parent's Motto: I Won't Give Up on You	Life's Little Challenges
You Bring A Lot To The Party	My Sister	Who Are You?
Nicole		

Game Instructions

Purpose: To discuss the meaning and impact of various poems.

Time: 90 minutes

People Needed: 6 to 8 of your closest friends

Materials Needed: One copy of each poem, pens, a handout with questions guests will respond to and writing paper.

Setting: an afternoon or evening with light refreshments or hors d'oeuvres, soothing music and comfortable environment. If possible, arrange seating so everyone is in a circle.

Preparation: invitations announcing a casual evening with friends, one copy of each poem and read all poems before playing The Game. The host or hostess is the facilitator for The Game and should read all poems before guests arrive.

Getting Started:

1) As friends arrive, state purpose is to play The Game. Describe The Game as a discussion about life experiences and issues are reflected in a collection of poetry.

2) Encourage friends to socialize, get refreshments and find a comfortable seat.

3) Once seated, give guests instructions. Explain that their task is for each person to select one title (game piece) from the bag. Once a game piece is selected, each person reads the title on the game piece and is given the appropriate poem. Each person should read their own poem. Ask everyone to be prepared to respond to the questions on the handout.

4) Allow 4 to 5 minutes for everyone to read and think about the poem.

5) Ask for a volunteer to read their poem aloud. Ask others to listen and think about what the writer is saying. Ask the reader to respond to the following questions first: What is the writer saying? What was your first impressions when you read this poem? How does the poem make you feel? Can you relate personally to this poem? If yes, please describe your experience. Please share any other thoughts about the poem. Read the author's interpretation after each poem is read.

6) After the reader had finished, ask for another volunteer and repeat step 5 until everyone has completed this step.

7) After everyone has read their poems and responded to the questions, ask everyone what they liked about the game and how they could make it better. You may also ask what this experience meant to them.

8) End the evening on positive them. Suggestions include: 1) Give out door prizes, 2) Lost of hugs, 3) Positive affirmations and 4) Schedule another day to play The Game.

Printed in the United States
by Baker & Taylor Publisher Services